Wavelets of Purpose

~ Ripples to Inspire Your Dreams into Reality ~

Wavelets of Purpose

~ Ripples to Inspire Your Dreams into Reality ~

H. JAMES WILLIAMS

WAVELETS OF PURPOSE
~ Ripples to Inspire Your Dreams into Reality ~

ISBN 13:   978-0-98343-420-7
ISBN 10:   0-983434-20-4

LCCN: 2011904690

Copyright (c) 2011
H. James Williams

To purchase additional books:
www.aliantsecuritygroup.org
800.764.7114

Cover Design & Printing by:
Anointed Press Graphics, Inc.
www.anointedpressgraphics.com
copyright (c) 2011

This book was printed in the United States of America. All rights reserved under United States of America Copyright Law. This book or parts thereof may not be reproduced in any form or by any means - electronic, mechanical, photocopy, recording or otherwise - without prior written permission of the publisher, except as provided by United States of America Copyright Law.

Dedication

Wavelets of Purpose is dedicated to that which is all-powerful and at the heart of all creation and purpose. This book is also dedicated to those who summon the faith and courage to act on the empowerment of creation and purpose that lies within each of us.

Acknowledgments

I wish to acknowledge the Creator without whose blessings Wavelets of Purpose would have become possible.

In loving memory of my parents.

To my children, grandchildren, siblings and in-laws with love.

To my teachers, students, friends and clients who are derivative sources of inspiration for this book's content.

To Anointed Press Publishers for their consultations and publishing.

Recommended Uses for Wavelets of Purpose To Inspire Your Dreams

Use the affirmations and reflections within Wavelets of Purpose to personally meditate and focus on issues, challenges and circumstances you wish to overcome or goals you wish to achieve in your life. Be sure to clear your mind and environment of unwanted distractions to be in tune to receive inward direction and personal clarity for yourself.

Use the appropriate affirmations and reflections as reminders of what you can achieve with good and purposeful determination regardless of circumstance. Use the affirmations to jump-start, formulate and write your own personal affirmations as you gain further clarity about what the affirmations contained in this book specifically mean to you.

Use the book's content for perpetual daily or weekly affirmations of purpose. Use the book in support and focus groups to provoke discussion and clarity about purpose and what it means for individual, familial, group or organizational purpose. Focus on the fact that ripples of water radiate in concentric circles with kinetic energy within a pond when graced by a pebble in motion. You need only be receptive to the wave of purpose generated by the creative force meant to launch your imbedded dreams into reality. Your purpose in life awaits the actions, affirmations and determination required by you for you to materialize your heaven sent dreams into reality.

Introduction

In the pursuit of wisdom, I am always on the lookout for ripples of knowledge that inspire the mind and soul to constructive purpose. Wavelets of Purpose comprises just a few ripples of wording that hopefully will speak more to the reader than the brevity of the words themselves for achieving purpose.

Everyone is ushered into this world and ends up serving some purpose not always fully understood at the time of its undertaking. Your life lived and completed will bear final testimony to the purpose it served. May this book inspire you to good purpose and the celebration of accomplished outcomes.

H. James Williams

Table of Contents

Ripples of Creation 15

Ripples of Life 25

Ripples of Character 33

Ripples of Commitment 39

Ripples of Planning 45

Ripples of Knowledge 53

Ripples of Friendship 59

Ripples of Action 65

Ripples of Service 73

Ripples of Accomplishments................................ 81

Ripples of CREATION

All endeavors of purpose are in accordance with the Creator's willingness for their accomplishment.

Ripples of Creation

Creation does not give you a vision without the time and means for the fulfillment of its purpose.

Love is the embodiment of creation and the human motivation for purpose.

Vision is the lamp that lights the pathways of purpose for all who are inspired to journey along any of its given paths.

Purpose and vision see where others for the moment are unable to see. For those who do see: action, ability and commitment entwined with faith are essentials needed for focusing the unseen into reality.

Ripples of Creation

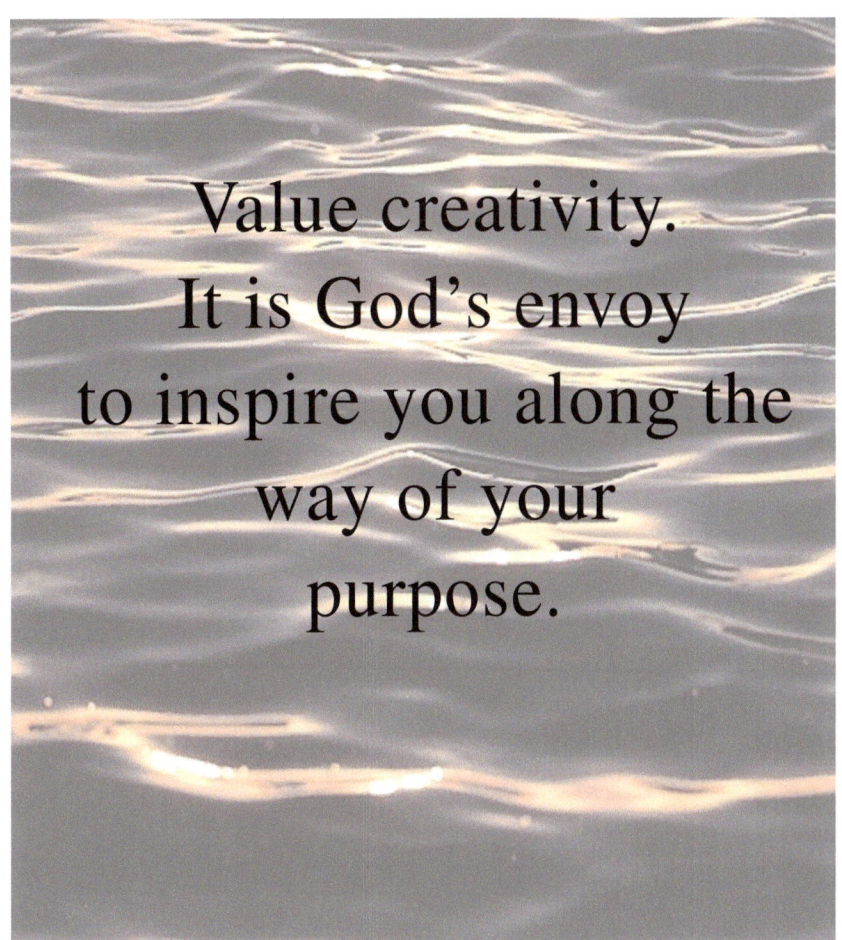

Value creativity.
It is God's envoy
to inspire you along the
way of your
purpose.

Imagination is the art of life and the wellspring of all purpose.

Ripples of Creation

We are each the agents of individually inspired purpose for accomplishing the collective purpose of the universe.

Ripples of

LIFE

A woman is God's instrument for wroughting His purpose in the world. It is through a woman that the miracle of life is achieved through conception and birth: the starting point of all potential for purpose.

Ripples of Life

You are what is within you, and
what is within you was presented to you through the ages through that which dwelled within those who lived before you.

Walk daily in the direction of your life's compelling true purpose.

Seeds of potentiality within us all only need to be nurtured for purposeful harvest.

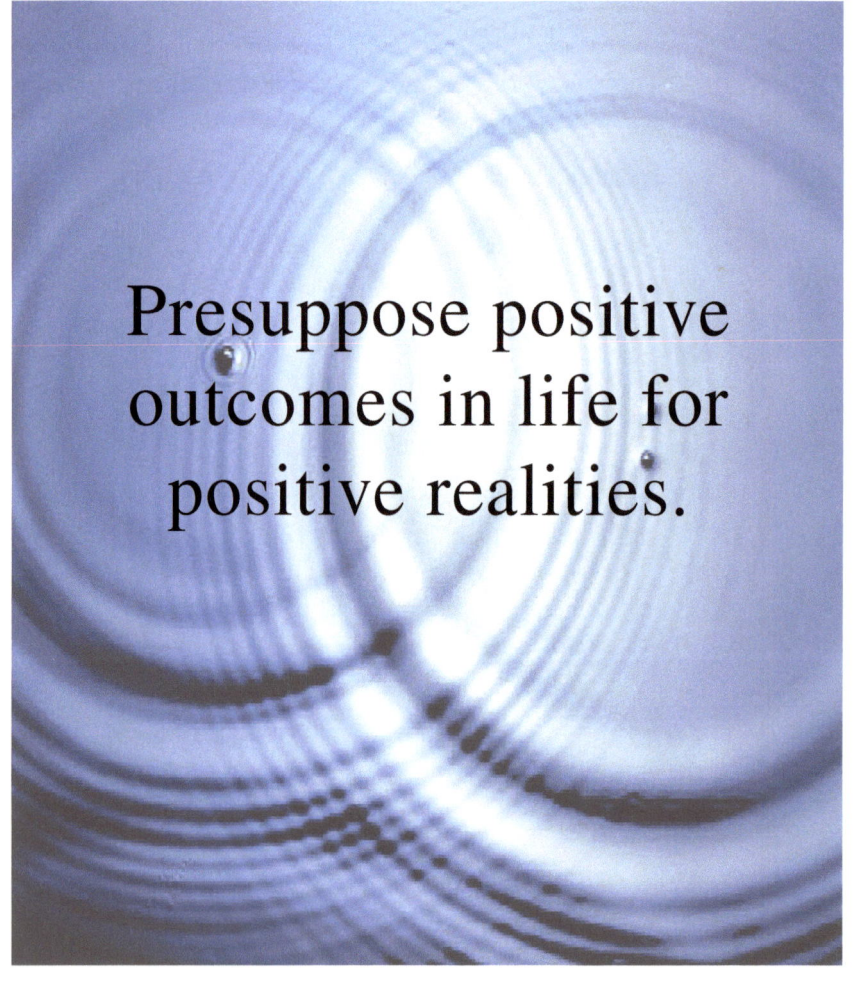

Presuppose positive outcomes in life for positive realities.

Who you are today is only a milestone toward becoming who you will allow yourself to become with each tomorrow.

The life you live is your sermon to others and the testimony of your purpose.

Ripples of

CHARACTER

What you cannot master has the ability to master you, but the power that resides within you has dominion to master all.

Ripples of Character

Your purpose will surface according to your values, motivation, abilities and behavior. Clarify and know yourself for its recognition and achievement.

It is better to love a purpose of good endeavor than to lust aimlessly after temporal gratification of the senses.

Monitor and control your senses for fear that any one of your senses gains the power to adversely control you.

Ripples of Character

Character knocks and takes up residency when integrity is at home. Purpose is weighed by honorable character for conducting business in all quarters.

Ripples of

COMMITMENT

The dream of becoming an oak tree first begins with the potential and belief of the acorn.

A stepping stone of committed purpose is able to overcome any mountain of doubt or fear.

Naked truth fears no challenge, and there is no true purpose that can prevail over time without it.

Human determination is extraordinary. It is the mental muscle and human mettle for overcoming challenges to purpose.

At times, adversity comes to prepare us for opportunities and purposes yet to be manifested and realized.

Ripples of

Planning

Seasons are all around us in nature and in life with each season of a thing having its own cycle of life and purpose.

Ripples of Planning

The power of the moment lies within its momentary decisions. Each decision of purpose becomes the foundation for the next.

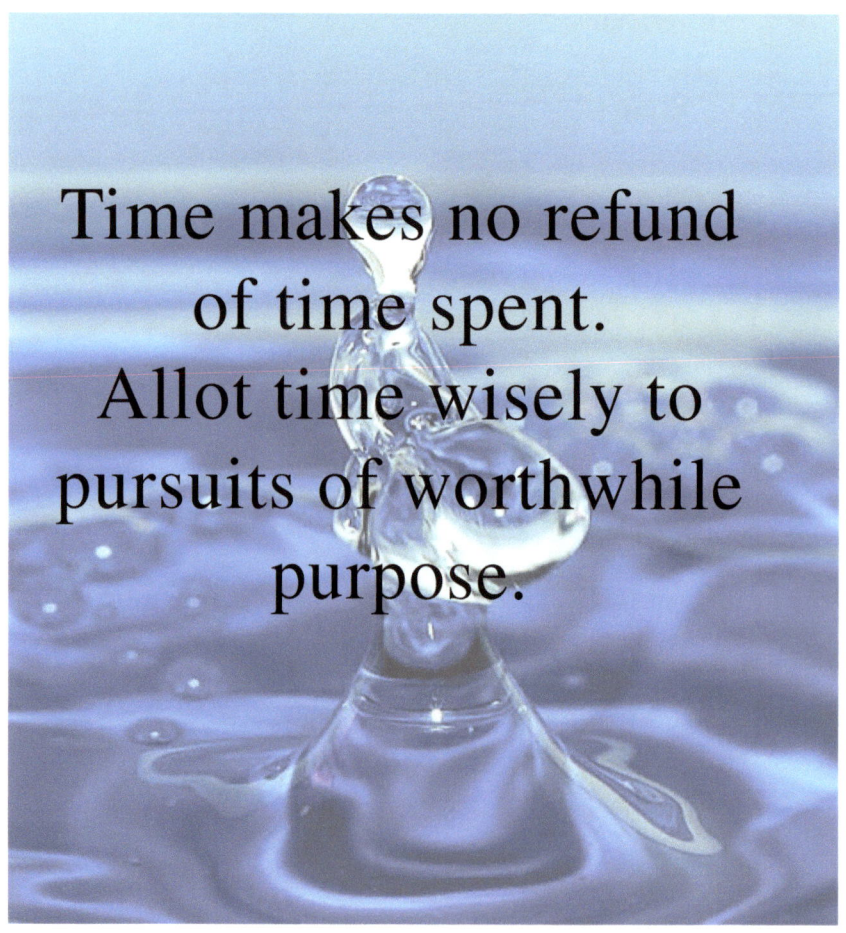

Time makes no refund of time spent. Allot time wisely to pursuits of worthwhile purpose.

Management controls purpose.
Leadership inspires purpose.

Plan well, perform well and treat others well in order to live well and excel.

Resist attempting goals
without direction
and a process for their
accomplishment.
To attempt otherwise is
to risk losing your way in
the tasks before you.

The underlying structure of individual purpose is only as secure as its foundation of commitment and ability: hence, the need to plan well.

Ripples of

KNOWLEDGE

Meaningful inquiry is
the key that
unlocks and determines
clear purpose.

Ripples of Knowledge

Everything in life offers a coaching session and enlightens a life lesson.

Age is the companion of wisdom,
spiritual knowledge and personal growth.

Ripples of Knowledge

Learn from challenges and problems faced, analyze and act with reason from lessons learned and celebrate accomplishments.

Knowledge for a purpose that is not acted upon becomes knowledge for a purpose ignored and its dream deferred.

Ripples of

FRIENDSHIP

Solitude harbors perception and clarity. The trusted friend and purpose come together to influence reason and action.

Honorable purpose is an alliance with another, or others, for good.

We become either rich or poor in spirit depending on the cause of our purpose and the people we keep by our side.

Physical union is temporal. Spiritual mental bonding is sacred. The spiritual mental bond collaboratively defines and achieves mutual purpose for accomplishment.

Ripples of

ACTION

To merely fantasize is to forsake genuine effort to bring your dreams into reality.

Ripples of Action

Words speak to dreams, but acts of love inspire and bring purposeful dreams into fruition.

Purpose finds the way. Fear and doubt make the excuse.

Each day is presented as a gift to continue along the path of your intended divine purpose.

Act consciously to have your dreams materialize according to your purpose. Do nothing in the pursuit of your dreams to have but a purpose unfulfilled.

Dreams with hope for tomorrow are transformed into existence by your actions taken today.

Ripples of

SERVICE

Service to your purpose for the moment may be preparing you for your ultimate life purpose.

Good purpose comes through you and not from you.
You are bestowed with talents and abilities to be used in service to others.

Purpose does not guarantee material or financial wealth. Purpose is having passion and ability to do what you are inwardly inspired to do in service to others for mankind's benefit.

To serve others in love,
is to glorify
your divine spirit.
To serve yourself
selfishly, is to glorify the
mistaken perception
of your carnal reality.

Love along the way of your course of good purpose in order to leave a path for others to find their way.

Bury not your purpose in the sand lest it be discovered and treasured by another for action leaving you to uselessly cry to the stars that you were beaten and robbed of your inheritance.

Ripples of

ACCOMPLISHMENT

Good purpose has its rewards, accolades and celebrations.
Give thanks and praise for accomplishments.

We are born into the light
of our day.
When our light of day
comes to its end,
we pass on into the
shadow of our night
where our day's efforts
will illuminate our night
as our star of purpose
among the heaven's stars.

Summary

Li fe involves listening and learning to clarify what is important to us. Doing so allows us to ultimately determine what purposes we choose to act on for living. Without a clear vision for living, one loses passion and enthusiasm to live productively. Your belief system, values, ability and association with others will strongly influence the course you choose to pursue in life. Commit and plan worthwhile endeavors with the support of an encouraging network of friends and resources and you will be well on your way to taking positive steps toward the accomplishment of your most cherished dreams. It is my wish for you that Wavelets of Purpose has been useful in thought and inspiration and that it will continually accompany you toward ever enriching possibilities of purpose and achievement.

About the Author

H. James Williams is a certified personal life coach. He is the owner of Aliant Coaching Services and coaches individuals of all ages who are seeking personal and professional transformational changes in their lives.

The affirmations and reflections used in Wavelets of Purpose are drawn from Mr. Williams' life coaching insights that have helped to constructively clarify and move clients toward their goals and desired outcomes. He hopes these same affirmations and reflections will provoke thought, conviction and action for you to do the same.

For more information about Aliant Coaching Services or any H. James Williams products or services, go to www.aliantsecuritygroup.org.

Aliant Security Group
DBA: Aliant Coaching Services
2702 Lighthouse Point East, Suite 621
Baltimore, Maryland 21224

To purchase additional books:
www.aliantsecuritygroup.org
800.764.7114

www.ingramcontent.com/pod-product-compliance
Lightning Source LLC
Chambersburg PA
CBHW041522090426
42737CB00037B/4